RELAXED COLORING

new seasons®
a division of Publications International, Ltd.

Let's get social!

 @Publications_International

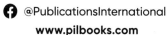 @PublicationsInternational

www.pilbooks.com

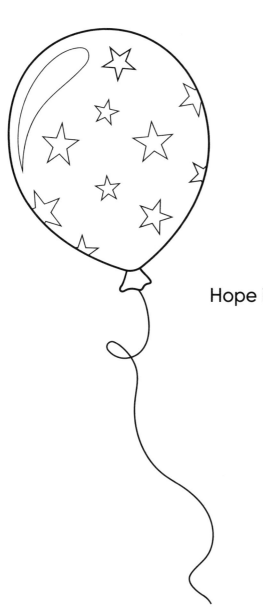

Hope is a waking dream.
—Aristotle

The Sun himself is weak when he first rises, and gathers strength and courage as the day gets on.

–Charles Dickens

When you own your breath, nobody can steal your peace.

—Anonymous

I know that you don't believe it, but indeed,
life will bring you through. You will live it down in time.
What you need now is fresh air, fresh air, fresh air!

—Fyodor Dostoevsky

The gentle bird can teach a lesson
you will be wiser and better for.

—Louisa May Alcott

A tune is more lasting than
the song of the birds,
and a word is more lasting
than the wealth of the world.

—Irish Proverb

Let your life lightly dance on the edges of time
like dew on the tip of a leaf.

—Rabindranath Tagore

Nature's peace will flow into you as sunshine flows into trees.
The winds will blow their own freshness into you, and the storms
their energy, while cares will drop off like autumn leaves.

—John Muir

To reach a port we must sail, sometimes with the wind, and sometimes against it. But we must not drift or lie at anchor.

—Oliver Wendell Holmes Sr.

Be thou the rainbow in the storms of life.
The evening beam that smiles the clouds away,
and tints tomorrow with prophetic ray.

—Lord Byron

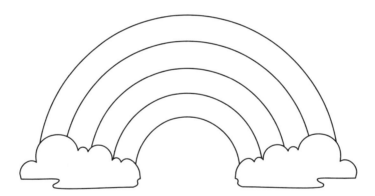

Knock on the sky and listen to the sound.

—Zen Proverb

Live in the sunshine,
swim the sea,
drink the wild air.

—Ralph Waldo Emerson

Look up, laugh loud, talk big, keep the color in your cheek
and the fire in your eye, adorn your person,
maintain your health, your beauty and your animal spirits.

—William Hazlitt

Look at the sparrows;
they do not know what they will do in the next moment.
Let us literally live from moment to moment.

—Mahatma Gandhi

Animals are such agreeable friends—
they ask no questions, they pass no criticisms.

—George Eliot

A smile cures the wounding of a frown.

—William Shakespeare

If you look the right way, you can see that the whole world is a garden.

—Frances Hodgson Burnett

The best portion of a good man's life: his little, nameless unremembered acts of kindness and love.

—William Wordsworth

Where love reigns, the impossible may be attained.

—Indian Proverb

Where there's hope, there's life. It fills us with fresh courage
and makes us strong again.

—Anne Frank

Hope is patience with the lamp lit.

—Tertullian

Surely there is something in the unruffled calm of
nature that overawes our little anxieties and doubts:
the sight of the deep-blue sky, and the clustering stars above,
seem to impart a quiet to the mind.

—Jonathan Edwards

Thousands of candles can be lighted from a single candle,
and the life of the candle will not be shortened.
Happiness never decreases by being shared.

—Buddha

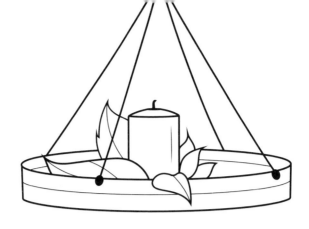

With freedom, flowers, books, and the moon,
who could not be perfectly happy?

—Oscar Wilde

The richness I achieve comes from nature,
the source of my inspiration.

—Claude Monet

There is a serene and settled majesty to woodland scenery
that enters into the soul and delights and elevates it,
and fills it with noble inclinations.

—Washington Irving

The best time to plant a tree was 20 years ago.
The second best time is now.

—Chinese Proverb

Keep your face always toward the sun—
and shadows will fall behind you.

—Walt Whitman

"On with the dance, let the joy be unconfined!" is my motto, whether there's any dance to dance or any joy to unconfine.

—Mark Twain

Never be in a hurry; do everything quietly and in a calm spirit. Do not lose your inner peace for anything whatsoever, even if your whole world seems upset.

—Saint Francis de Sales

In calmness lies true pleasure.

—Victor Hugo

You must live in the present, launch yourself on every wave, find your eternity in each moment.

—Henry David Thoreau

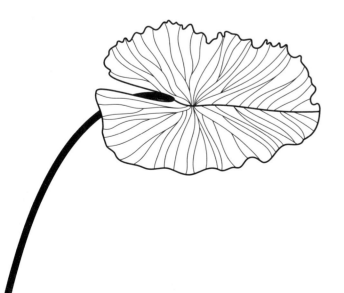

What is love without passion? —A garden without flowers,
a hat without feathers, tobogganing without snow.

—Jennie Jerome Churchill

No man can paddle two canoes at the same time.

—Bantu Proverb

No human being, however great, or powerful, was
ever so free as a fish.

—John Ruskin

It is extraordinary to see the sea; what a spectacle!
She is so unfettered that one wonders whether it is
possible that she again become calm.

—Claude Monet

You cannot perceive beauty but with a serene mind.

—Henry David Thoreau

Our greatest experiences are our quietest moments.

—Friedrich Nietzsche

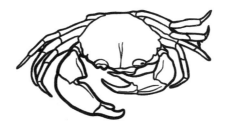

Peace cannot be kept by force; it can only be achieved by understanding.

—Albert Einstein

Your mind will answer most questions if you learn to relax and wait for the answer.

—William Burroughs

There is no shame in not knowing;
the shame lies in not finding out.

—Russian Proverb

It is often the small steps, not the giant leaps,
that bring about the most lasting change.

—HRM Queen Elizabeth II

One day or day one.
It's your choice.

—Anonymous

When I let go of what I am,
I become what I might be.

—Lao Tzu

Be where you are;
otherwise you will miss your life.

—Buddha

To lie sometimes on the grass under trees on a summer's day, listening to the murmur of the water, or watching the clouds float across the sky, is by no means a waste of time.

—Sir John Lubbock

Energy is eternal delight.

—William Blake

The heart that loves is always young.

—Greek Proverb

He who is of calm and happy nature will hardly feel the pressure of age, but to him who is of an opposite disposition, youth and age are equally a burden.

—Plato

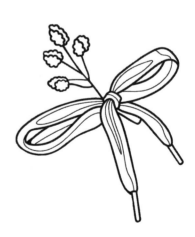

There is only one happiness in life,
to love and be loved.

—George Sand

Hope is that place
that lies between
dreaming and doing.

—Anonymous

How beautiful it is to do nothing,
and then to rest afterwards.

—Spanish Proverb

Go wisely and slowly.
Those who rush stumble and fall.

—William Shakespeare

Invest in rest.

—Anonymous

There are moments when all anxiety and stated toil are becalmed in the infinite leisure and repose of nature.

—Henry David Thoreau

Health and cheerfulness
mutually beget each other.

—Joseph Addison

Rest and be thankful.

—William Wordsworth

Yesterday is ashes, tomorrow wood.
Only today does the fire burn brightly.

—Inuit Proverb

As rain falls equally on the just and the unjust, do not burden your heart with judgments but rain your kindness equally on all.

—Buddha

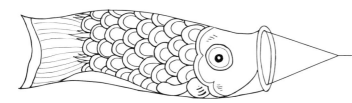

No act of kindness, no matter how small,
is ever wasted.

—Aesop

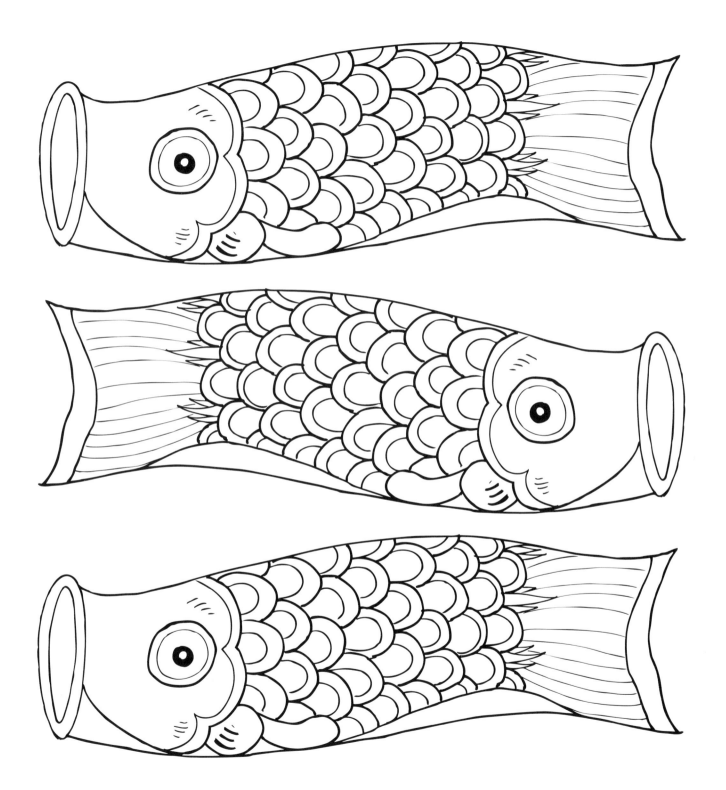

If you want to go fast, go alone. If you want to go far, go together.

—African Proverb

I often think that the night is more alive
and more richly colored than the day.

—Vincent van Gogh

Write it on your heart that every day is
the best day in the year.

–Ralph Waldo Emerson